Jean McNeil is originally from Nova Scotia, Canada, but has lived in London for twenty years. She is the author of nine books, including four novels and a collection of short fiction. She is the recipient of several international fellowships and has recently undertaken residencies in the Arctic and in the Falkland Islands. She teaches on the MA in Creative Writing at the University of East Anglia and at Birkbeck College in London.

Also by Jean McNeil

From the Library of Graham Greene
The Rough Guide to Costa Rica
Hunting Down Home
Nights in a Foreign Country
Private View
The Interpreter of Silences
The Ice Diaries: Antarctic work-in-progress
The Ice Lovers

NIGHT ORDERS
POEMS FROM
ANTARCTICA AND THE ARCTIC

Jean McNeil

Writer-in-residence
Environment Institute • UCL
2009-2010

First published in Great Britain by

Smith/Doorstop Books
The Poetry Business
Bank Street Arts
32-40 Bank Street
Sheffield S1 2DS

and the Environment Institute Press
at the Environment Institute
University College London
Gower Street
WC1E 6BT
in 2011

Copyright © Jean McNeil 2011
The moral right of the author has been asserted.
All rights reserved.

The right of Jean McNeil to be identified as the author of this work has been asserted in accordance with the Copyright, Designs and Patents Act 1988.

This book is sold subject to the condition that it shall not, by way of trade or otherwise, be lent, resold, hired out or otherwise circulated without the publisher's prior consent in any form of binding or cover other than that in which it is published and without a similar condition including this condition being imposed on the subsequent purchaser.

A CIP record for this book is available from the British Library

ISBN 978 906613 39 6

Printed on recycled paper by Antony Rowe CPI Ltd.
Designed and set by Kate Kirkwood
Front and back cover photos © Tim Page

Smith/Doorstop Books are a member of Inpress:
www.inpressbooks.co.uk
Distributed by Central Books Ltd., 99 Wallis Road, London E9 5LN

The Poetry Business is an Arts Council National Portfolio Organisation

Contents

Acknowledgements / vi
Foreword – Mark Ford / viii
Introduction / 1

ANTARCTICA

Notebook – November 28th, 2005 / 10
The Stanley Planetary Model Walk / 11
Edvard Munch/38 Fitzroy Road/Conductivity / 14
Ship Diary / 16
Glacier 11pm / 21
Ice Observations / 22
Running out of Night / 27
Night Flight, March 5th / 34
Notebook – March 14th, 2006 / 36
The Antarctic Convergence / 37
Ice Diaries / 47
Endurance / 59

ARCTIC

Notebook – August 15th, 2009 / 62
Two Sunrises / 63
Letter to the Shadow Man / 64
Notebook, August 20th, 2009 / 66
Night Orders / 67
69° North / 72
Nansen / 73
Isfjord / 74
Notebook – September 2nd, 2009 / 76
Arctic Pilot / 78
Kap Farvel / 85

Acknowledgements

These poems were written under the aegis of two polar residencies: as the British Antarctic Survey/Arts Council of England International Fellow in Antarctica, November 2005-April 2006, and as writer-in-residence aboard the Natural Environment Research Council's science cruise JR175 to Greenland, aboard the Royal Research Ship *James Clark Ross*, August-September 2009.

I would like to thank the British Antarctic Survey and Arts Council England for providing me with such a unique opportunity as a writer, and for their subsequent support. My thanks also go to Professor Mark Maslin, former Director of the Environment Institute at University College London for his stalwart support, without which this book would not have been possible. I would also like to thank Mark Ford of University College London's English Department, for providing an introduction. Thanks too to the Natural Environment Research Council and especially to Colm O'Cofaigh of Durham University for agreeing to host me aboard JR175, and to Captain Jerry Burgan of the *James Clark Ross* for his help in writing 'Arctic Pilot'. For 'Night Orders'; the text in italics is taken from the logbook of the *James Clark Ross*, Voyage 18, entries written by Jerry Burgan. My thanks also go to Kate Kirkwood for her elegant text and cover design.

Earlier versions of 'Glacier, 11pm', 'Ice Observations', a previous version of 'Ice Diaries', 'Running out of Night' and 'The Antarctic Convergence' have been previously published in a limited edition booklet of Antarctic work-in-progress, *The Ice Diaries*, 2006. An earlier version of 'Arctic Pilot' appears in the online literary magazine and literary website of Birkbeck College at the University of London, The Writer's Hub: www.writershub.net. 'Endurance' was published in *Prism International* vol 49: 3, Spring 2011.

A note on texts used in these poems • In 'Running out of Night', definitions of ice types are from The World Meteorological Organisation's SEA-ICE NOMENCLATURE. ILLUSTRATED GLOSSARY WMO/OMM/ – No.259 • Edition 1970–2004. *www.aari.nw.ru/.../nomenclature/WMO_Nomenclature_draft_version1-0.pdf*

'Arctic Pilot' and 'Isfjord' contain short extracts from the *British Admiralty Sailing Directions* Arctic Pilot Vol. III, 8th (2007) Edition – NP 12. © Crown Copyright and/or database rights. Reproduced by permission of the Controller of Her Majesty's Stationery Office and the UK Hydrographic Office (www.ukho.gov.uk)

Photo credits • All images in this book are mine with the exception of the following: Cover images courtesy of Tim Page; Antarctic map © Mapping and Geographic Information Centre, British Antarctic Survey; Stanley Solar System Sculpture drawings are by the designer and sculptor R. Yssel; JR175 (Greenland) cruise track and swath images courtesy of Colm O'Cofaigh and Jerry Burgan; Ilulissat iceberg courtesy of Jerry Burgan.

Foreword

Thirty-three miners, at the time I'm writing this, are trapped underground in a mine in Chile. It was initially assumed that they had all died, but two and a half weeks after the mine's collapse a rescue mission picked up a faint tapping, and it was discovered they had somehow found refuge in a cave the size of a one-bedroom flat, and survived on a teaspoonful of canned tuna and a couple of sips a water a day. The rejoicing of their relatives was soon, alas, tempered by the news that it was going to take three or four months for engineers to drill down through the rock and excavate a shaft up which their loved ones could be winched to safety. In an attempt to understand the psychological challenges the miners' prolonged stay in such cramped, lightless conditions would pose, BBC Radio 4's *Today* programme contacted Patrick Power of the British Antarctic Survey; he was in the middle of an eighteen-month stint at the South Pole, and described what it was like to live isolated in a group through the dark, stormy, freezing (ie. below minus 40) Antarctic winter. 'It can be quite an intense experience,' is how he summed it up.

Jean McNeil's *Night Orders* assembles photographs, poems and prose pieces that vividly convey her 'intense experience' of both the Antarctic and the Arctic. She spent three and a half months in Antarctica with the British Antarctic Survey, and in 2009 joined a scientific expedition off the western coast of Greenland. In recent years numerous writers have paid visits to these hostile regions, normally as part of an effort to publicise the effects of global warming. In *Night Orders* McNeil refers only obliquely to the changes wrought in the ice caps by the inexorable rise in world temperatures; hers is not a book with a 'message', but an attempt to render the psychological effects of the kinds of deprivation, and exhilaration, entailed by months spent surrounded by ice and snow.

The threat of the ice caps' melting, and the devastation this would unleash, has made your average news-consumer think of Antarctica as somehow more fragile, less implacable than when such as Scott and Shackleton and Amundsen ventured there some 100 years ago. 'Deep Field', a chapter in the long sequence 'Ice Diaries', offers a sharp correction to any such tendencies: it describes a blizzard in all its ferocity; a whiteout in which to venture even sixty feet from camp is to court death; a pure cold whose 'fiery quartz spears' the mind can barely process. It also initiates the romance that acts as a narrative thread binding together the succession of polar days, and that colours the 'blank hours' of McNeil's life in this monochrome world.

The extremes of such locations inevitably generate an extreme kind of verbal texturing. Surveying a barren winter scene in his great poem 'The Snow Man', the American poet Wallace Stevens declared one must develop 'a mind of winter' to respond fully to complete absence; by inuring himself to cold and emptiness, the speaker imagines himself becoming 'nothing himself', and then beholding 'Nothing that is not there and the nothing that is'. In *Night Orders* McNeil gives us plenty of details about the social life of the Survey and the ship on which she travelled to Greenland, but one never quite forgets the sublime distances dwarfing the fragile huts and vessels that shelter her, the endless featureless horizons, and 'the lure of denial', to use her own phrase, such landscapes inspire.

Mark Ford
September 2010

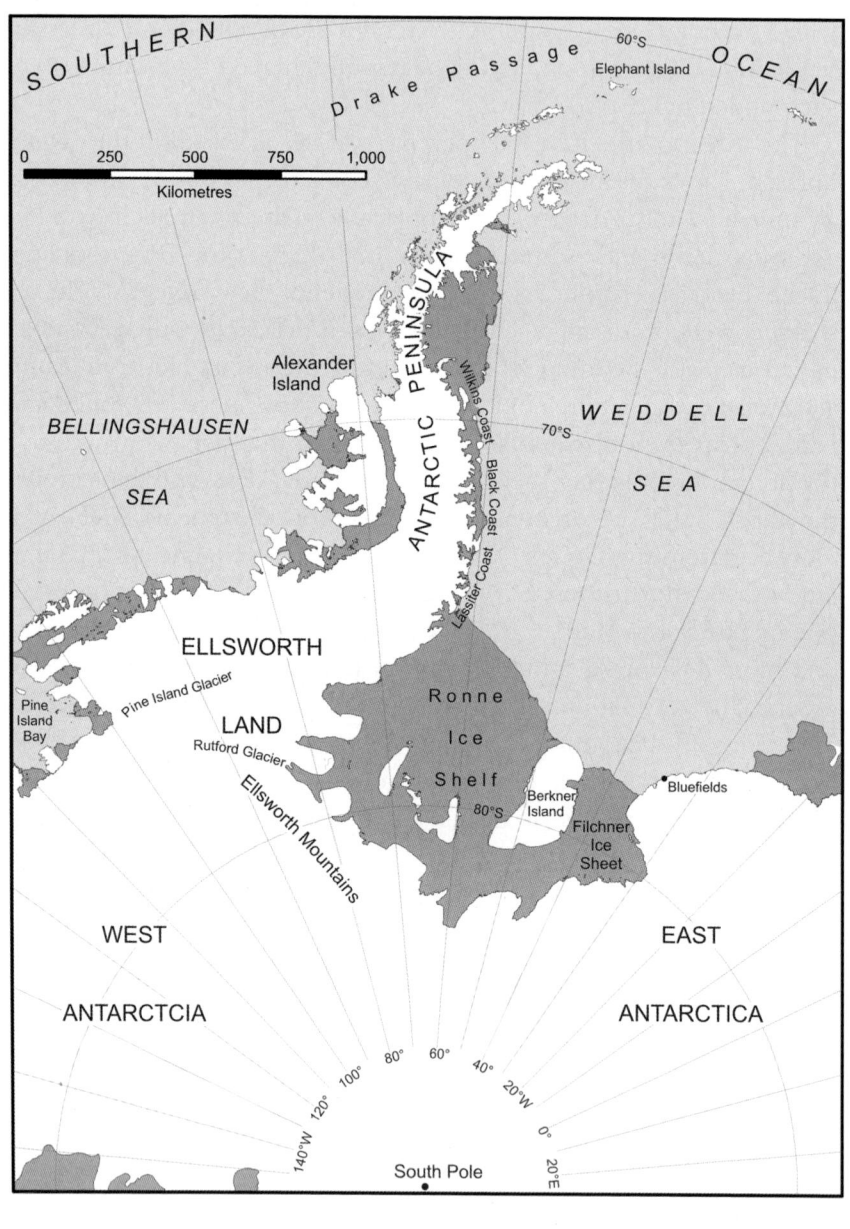

Introduction

Even in the 21st Century there is an epic quality to a journey to the Antarctic. We left London on 24th November 2005, leaving behind a darkening winter and journeying into a burst of day which would not be extinguished until late the following February. First our motley crew of British Antarctic Survey scientists and technical support people – plumbers, mechanics, builders – flew to Madrid, then overnight to Santiago de Chile, where we spent another night before flying the following day to the Falkland Islands via Puerto Montt and Punta Arenas. By the time we arrived on the wind-slashed tarmac at Mount Pleasant (a misnomer if there ever was one), the British Forces airport on East Falkland, I felt each of the 12,000-plus kilometres we had flown on this circuitous route.

We were supposed to spend only a few days in the Falklands before boarding our ship to the Antarctic, but as often happens in Antarctica, plans change. The ship was late coming from South Georgia, and my first experience of the Antarctic was this scrappy archipelago (over 740 landmasses make up the islands) at the bottom of the Atlantic which BAS personnel come to know chiefly as an antechamber to the frozen continent, but whose sternness and peculiarity captivated me on its own terms.

Finally we boarded our ship. We staggered across the Drake Passage, spending about half the time stationary as the oceanographers on board conducted CTDs, or Conductivity, Thermal and Depth analyses of the ocean currents. Between the CTD schedule and cargo-ing in a base, Port Lockroy, as well as a technical call into Vernadsky, the Ukrainian base, what is normally a four or five day straight passage to the Antarctic became first eleven days, then thirteen, then, as our ship was beset by pack ice, longer. For a while then it was unclear if we would actually reach our destination at all at Rothera, the main scientific base of the British Antarctic Survey, tucked away on a hook-shaped point on the lee side of Adelaide Island, about half way down the Antarctic Peninsula.

But we did arrive, by the skin of our teeth. And there I stayed, leaving only occasionally to fly out to Sky Blu, a blue ice runway and refuelling station down on the ice cap near Ellsworth Land, or on 'local area familiarisation flights' around the immediate area, or to go out in Rigid Inflatable Boats (RIBs) to help with oceanographic and marine biology surveys.

I was sent to the Antarctic thanks to the British Antarctic Survey and the Arts Council England, which together for ten years ran a competitive fellowship to the Antarctic for visual artists and writers. This polar notebook charts that first journey to the Antarctic, which ended when all of us summer personnel left on the last ship of the season on April 4th 2006, and also a return journey of sorts, this time to its mirror opposite, the Arctic – specifically the west coast of Greenland – in the summer of 2009. In between these trips I undertook a residency in Spitsbergen, the main island of the Svalbard archipelago in the Norwegian Arctic in the summer of 2007 and have since returned to the Falklands three times, including a two month stay in 2008 under the auspices of an Arts Council England/ Shackleton Scholarship Fund grant. From these journeys I published two books out of my experience: *The Ice Diaries – Antarctic Work in Progress* (2006) and *The Ice Lovers*, a novel, in 2009. I also wrote a travel/memoir/meditation on ice, *Ice Diaries*, which remains unpublished.

This book, *Night Orders*, takes its title from the Master's logbook aboard the *James Clark Ross*, the Natural Environment Research Council-owned scientific research ship on which I journeyed to the Antarctic and later to Greenland. The polar regions can be visited without ever stepping onto a ship, but for me the Antarctic and the Arctic are inextricably linked to the sea, and to the maritime history of polar explorations. Another abiding theme is the fantastical relationship between night and day. Those of us brought up in the temperate regions are programmed with an expectation of a certain diurnal and nocturnal regime. But the high latitudes of the Antarctic and the Arctic are all-or-nothing places; either there is too much light or too much night. This tilting between surfeit and lack communicates itself to us and provokes a similar emotional response – even already intense characters are taken to new extremities of feeling. The going-for-broke attitude of many of these poems is perhaps mawkish in places, but in the polar regions I found I cared little for a nuanced, intelligent, balanced approach to life. There, you are alive and just want to live. This seems – for once – enough.

The theme of night ripples through this collection. Night moves quickly – at the onset of the austral polar winter in March-April 2006 we lost nearly an hour of light each day at Rothera. This rapid repeal of light from the world triggered in me a kind of physical rather than psychological panic. This was one of many experiences which taught me how poorly I would fare compared to that generation of sailors and explorers who overwintered in the high latitudes. The polar night also taught me that to know light you must also know darkness, that extreme opposites are somehow two faces of a whole, and that the fantastical regimes of dark and light have internal as well as stellar and planetary rhythms. In the polar regions I tilted between euphoria and dread, and sometimes lost the struggle for equilibrium.

It was Steve the base commander who told me about the ice book. A strange little book, he said, was tucked away in the Rothera library. He'd had a look at it once, but then lost track of it. The book was an ice glossary – a list of all the different forms of ice, written for mariners. It was in the tradition of the books carried on ships, he said: glossaries of knots, or wind, or sea-faring terms.

A whole book on the language of ice. How many kinds of ice

could there be? There was ice, and there was snow. And that was about it.

After some rummaging in the dust-less library (the Antarctic is too dry to sustain dust mites, so no dust) I found the book. It was a thin paperback with blue paper covers; published in the 1950s, its covers were worn but not 'foxed', as they say in the book trade – those singed edges and brown liver spots which accumulate around the edges of papers and bindings – because in the Antarctic there is so little moisture in the air.

The book was called *A Glossary of Ice Terms*. They were typed out in the Courier of old typewriters: *Ablation, Black Ice, Frazil Ice, Candle Ice, First Year Ice, Glass Ice, Growler, Hummock, Ice Gruel, Pressure Ice, Rotten Ice, Sastrugi, Serac, Stamukha, Tarn, Winter Ice*. There would be more to learn about ice than I had thought.

Ice has a life cycle, just as we do. We talk of it living and dying, when it melts. But technically ice is immortal; it never quite dies but is transformed, through melt, into water, into vapour. The Antarctic is by far the largest accumulation of ice on earth. Along with Greenland, the Antarctic ice sheet is the most complete frozen archive of our planet's past. The great ice sheets are also oracles, however reluctant or accidental. Ice provides a precise record of the atmospheric past through the chemical residues it traps, and in particular how the planet has responded to past episodes of warming and cooling. Through analysing this data, scientists can offer a likely scenario of how climate cycles and man-made emissions will affect the temperature of the planet.

As is often the case with writers, beneath the official narrative of a fellowship and a pseudo-scholarly investigation of ice was a personal story. Mine in the Antarctic in particular was one of love and loss – not bad material for a writer. There is another presence lurking outside the margins of these poems as much as it hovers at the margins of our perception. 'Why does everyone always think about God in the Antarctic?', an otherwise agnostic field assistant asked me.

Something in our isolation and vulnerability, married with the cold voltage of the place, lead one down the metaphysical path. There I felt – perhaps imagined is the better word – the presence of an indifferent will, vastly external to us and not at all preoccupied with our measly destinies.

Just by travelling to the polar regions one is enacting a pre-scripted story, of exploration and quest. In part it's an old instinct to venture over the edge of the known world and return, hopefully transformed by what you have found there. But now the planet is changing, and the polar regions took me to think deeply and subjectively about what ice might mean, to humans and human culture.

I was already familiar with ice. I grew up in Nova Scotia and New Brunswick on the east coast of Canada, where winter temperatures often dip below minus twenty degrees Celsius, and the windchill factor can drag them down much further. In fact the Antarctic was balmy compared to Canada, or so I thought until the Antarctic winter arrived. I spent many winters longing for an escape from cold, and did manage to break out of ice jail in my early twenties, when I came to live in the damp latitudes of the British isles. My time in the polar regions taught me to revalue the world of cold. We believe we are poised on the end of an era in our planet's history; the ice will go away. And with it what will it take? What do we stand to lose, in a world without ice?

For one, there is a lexicon at stake. This may not be everyone's priority, but as any writer knows the discovery of a new crop of words can provoke and inform a completely new artistic work.

Take the humble word iceberg – it comes from Dutch: *Ijs* = ice + *berg* = hill or mountain. Then there are more exotic words, such as *Polynya,* from the Russian, which means a polygon-shaped area of open water within pack ice. Much of the language used to describe the Antarctic is purloined from the Arctic and its various languages – a *nunatak,* for instance, meaning an isolated peak protruding above a surface of inland ice or snow, is Greenlandic; the Russian word *stamhuka* describes a thick piece of grounded hummock ice found in sea-ice; the sharp ridges formed by wind on snow surfaces are known by another Russian word, *sastrugi*. This is a lean lexicon, not two hundred years old; very few words are truly Antarctic in origin, and these are mainly naval or military terms, or taken from Australian English.

Other words are not about ice per se: *Southern aurora* – the auroral corona, the austral version of the northern lights; the *Crowberry*, a high-latitude berry which grows on the Falkland Islands and on Tristan de Cunha; *Diamond Dust* – tiny crystals of ice in cold air, brilliantly reflecting sunlight; *Diddle-dee* – a resinous small shrub native to the Falklands; *Gang line* – dog sledging, part of the harness to which sledge dogs were attached; *Glacieret* – miniature glacier, *Glory Hour* (Falklands): an hour of Sunday drinking at a public house; *Saints* – not, as you might think, an undiscovered pantheon of holy Antarctic men but the term for people from St Helena; *Big Eye* – insomnia attributed to changes in the length of daylight in Antarctic regions and finally *Antarcticitis* – a yearning for Antarctica. I also came to love those *f* and *s* words of glaciology, which is its own subsection of the language of ice: firn, flux, friction, shear, stress – for their medicinal, almost Greek tang.

On board the *JCR* in Greenland in 2009 I was surrounded by paleo-glaciologists and paleo-climatologists; the prefix indicates studiers of the very distant past. For paleo people, 8000 years ago was yesterday; they are much more interested in what happened to the great ice sheets 400,000 years ago. Human timescales became irrelevant, and humans too. Here I was introduced to an entirely new ecosystem distinct from the Antarctic; there were so many new cetaceans to get to grips with, for one: the Lesser Beaked Whale, Hectori's Beaked Whale, the Ginko-toothed Beaked Whale – more compelling names for creatures I had never known existed.

What follows is a journal, an account of the journey, and a struggle to apprehend and express in writing what I saw and felt in the polar regions. *Night Orders* is not structured like a conventional poetry collection which tends to place the strongest poems first and last; rather it moves chronologically, following each of the journeys I made and culminating in a major long sequence poem as the penultimate piece in each section. Many of the poems are little more than sketches and diary entries, sometimes accompanied by images.

Any writer setting foot on the Antarctic in particular is aware of the futility of being a writer on a continent wholly dedicated to scientific endeavour, and which comes with a literary legacy hard to live up to, in the form of the greatest explorer and expeditionary literature ever written. The Antarctic is a place which requires and rewards technical skill, physical stamina, and personal resourcefulness – not necessarily qualities associated with desk-bound writers. There is also a certain failure of language, when confronted with the continent's grandeur, its spectacularly aloof persona. In keeping with the Antarctic's documentary tradition I have sometimes used texts already extant – for example the Ice Gazetteer – and have often resorted to prose poetry, rather than poetry *per se*, in order to document the helix of emotion and fact I encountered in these regions.

More than anything, I gained in the Antarctic and Arctic a body of knowledge to do with polar science and Earth systems science in general, and an abiding love and feeling of – fraternity, stewardship, awe, a fierce unrequited love?; it's still not quite clear to me what to call this feeling – for the remaining great ice sheets of the world, which I have been so fortunate to witness. The poems and fragments here are verbal photographs of essentially mysterious places. As a book it is floating, adrift, perhaps because much of it was written on water. It is also unfinished and unfinishable – a subjective account of an ongoing journey.

ANTARCTICA

NOTEBOOK: NOVEMBER 28, 2005

Stanley, Falkland Islands

Colours: mustard • lead • tawny brown

The *QE II* is expected in today. Cruise ships consume the harbour. But we are going on a planet walk – this is one of the many quirks of this place, that around Stanley harbour are scattered models of the planets, at intervals which are to scale with the sun. The sun itself is plunked in front of a shipwreck called the *Jhelum*. The harbour is littered with rusting hulks. A nautical graveyard. I don't know why they have been left here to decay. Like many things in this place it seems to be symbolic somehow, along with the uncleared minefields. Gonzalo the Chilean bartender told me that mines have been left deliberately he thinks, *para que se recuerden* – so that the islanders remember.

The Stanley Planetary Model Walk

1.
He is the sun's own sign. Small bodies suffer
disparities of size and mass. Some planets
have little or no atmosphere. Some planets
get to you. We know planets revolve
endlessly in their orbits. We know we are here
only through luck. We ask will the earth
end in fire or ice, or simply wear away?

2.
As we were landing the plane was blown
sideways by a 45 knot gust. At the last
minute the pilot shoved the nose straight.
We took to it straight away, the toytown capital,
the ALERT STATE: BIKINI, the sheep-
and-Union Jack décor. Even the wounds of war:
skeletal helicopters, spent shells,
Argentinian toothpaste beneath a cairn
where some soldier years younger than him, even,
had died. Across the harbour two oil storage
containers squat like rusting cake tins. Shipwrecks
bleach in the Sound, storm-racked relics. After
surviving Cape Horn they were scuttled when
the islanders demanded ransom for their repair.

3.
Gunmetal rivers of stone flow down mustard hills.
Notes from a geological pamphlet:
periglacial blockfields, blockstreams

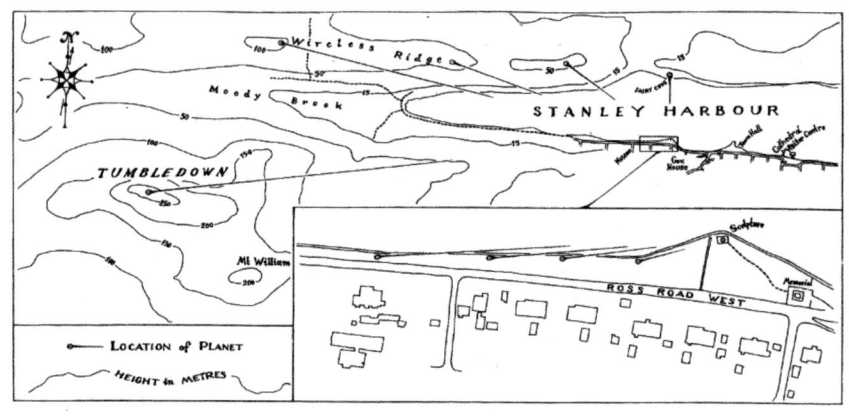

— L A Y ☉ U T —

	model size				real size			
speed round Sun in Cm/day	distance to Sun in metres	diameter in Cm			diameter in Km	distance to Sun in million Km	period round Sun	speed round Sun in thousand Km/hr
		139	SUN		1,392,539			
414	58	0.49	MERCURY		4,878	58	88 days	172
302	108	1.21	VENUS		12,104	108	228	126
258	150	1.28	EARTH		12,756	150	365.3	107
207	228	0.68	MARS		6,794	228	690	86
113	778	14.2	JUPITER		142,800	778	11.9 years	47
83	1,400	12	SATURN		120,000	1,400	29.5	34
59	2,870	5.2	URANUS		52,000	2,870	84	24
47	4,500	4.8	NEPTUNE		48,400	4,500	164	19
41	5,900	0.25	PLUTO		2,445	5,900	247	17
8 round Earth	0.4 to Earth	0.35	Moon		3,476	0.4 to Earth	27.3 days	3.7 round Earth

basalt, polerite relics of permafrost –
the orange hue comes from iron oxide.
The names of things here sound like gulps,
whale grass, darker ferns, Diddle-dee, the dip
and scarp of frost-shattered rocks of
gale-howled barrens. Sere horizons harried
by clouds. In the upside-down spring
November clouds of gorse fume coconut,
an ozone-less sun blares like Greece in summer.

4.
'Maths are not as abstract as people think,'
he says as we walk to the outer reaches
of the solar system; we want to see if Jupiter
has its moons. 'They're about how one thing
relates to another.' Stanley is on the same
latitude south as London is north: 52 degrees,
but here the light is a sword. Across the Sound
names of Navy destroyers that saved the islands
from bombardment are spelled out on the dun hills
in white stones: DEFENDER, ENDURANCE.
'That's one way to show your gratitude,' he says.
He gives supple explanations of hypsometry,
horizontal shear deformations, shallow-ice
equations. So, what's left? Will, the white bone
of desire, stringy thrust of sky. Ice, he says,
issues lateral warnings, old clues that say
something about burning. We walk, eating
chocolate mini-eggs from Pluto to Jupiter.

Edvard Munch/
38 Fitzroy Road/Conductivity

On our last night in the Falklands we host a dinner
of supermarket pizza and desiccated
pineapple. All day I have been reading
about Edvard Munch in the *London Review of Books*.
Edvard is fed up with rampant bohemia
the whole strata of it. Winter is the final
season. December is high summer
in the south Atlantic but today we had sleet.
In Oslo (then Kristiania) the painter
lours in black and white, his already mournful
face haggard with love. See him shuttle to dinner
parties where something always goes wrong,
someone — usually the most beautiful woman
at the table — says something cutting: *Edvard,
you have this useless instinct to feel
the pain.* He knows she is right and worse, she is
insulated from such random injustices
by her beauty. His paintings become stripped
of joy; in its place are stark white stripes
of anxiety. He wants to say: I know too much
already about life beneath the skin, how
criticism and intimacy run on the same
lurid current. I would like to reconsider
myself entirely. Too much of this life
has been about things not happening.
A dispute brews in his soul just like
the pub brawls down at the *Globe*. He feels
like flinging the wine glasses from the table.

But this is Oslo in 1902 and that
would be rude. Night lingers on our forgotten
latitude. Fingers chart table edges. Feel the
moment slide from your synapses, its dark allure.
The evening pewter harbour, our table
a wreck of empty bottles and pizza crusts.
Edvard looks on, horrified to find that
nothing has changed, that it is the same, even now –
these slippery dénouements of evenings
aborted forays into trusts into
the lavish mystery of the other.

Ship Diary

December 8th

Fourth day at sea. We cross a series of invisible
thresholds marked by a gelling of the world;
'growlers' appear first – submerged ice, the wreckage
of icebergs. Then pinnacle bergs, ghost ships
their spinnakers frozen into position.
We puncture the Antarctic Convergence
its boundary patrolled by 'tabs' –
tabular bergs.

These are lit from within like giant dioramas
a white-platinum lamp burning at their core they are
the least real thing I have ever seen in my life.

How many whites? The ivory of the old berg,
the bleached phosphorus glare of the ice sheet.
Transparent albumen of soaked ice,
dusk opal, albino, rose-grey,
the metallic blue-white of an electric current
or a lightning strike,
a pale dull jade.

In the sky, iceblink –
the reflection of pack ice on sky
strobe-lit, blank internal
lightning

December 9th

We spend the day
as disaster movie extras
fire drill, boat drill, casualty drill, finally
abandon ship drill.

We are spacemen. We take to the lifeboat, a self-righting vomitorium

immersion shock
is when the body suffers instant cardiac arrest.

The purser is Glaswegian. '*Brrrr*, iceberg!
Grrrrr Fire drill!
Muster point
Brrgggrrr all of yez!'

As it turns out, what we fear most on the ship is fire.
Fires rapidly become uncontainable
in an oxygen-rich environment.
We don smoke hoods
walk around the ship, suffocating amber glassine shields
that turn the world tobacco.

I dream that night of rogue waves;
once every nine wave cycles, the wave
which comes after is larger.
Nine is the beginning of one energy circuit,
and the end of another.

After dinner he appears in my door –
he is one of those people who never arrive
but land, like a spaceship. A dark spiral turns

at the heart of his every manoeuvre.
These people, I think, they have grace
but not kindness, as if physical beauty
cannot stand to be blunted.

It is not so easy to avoid truth here.
This is a new life, now. There is no escape.

December 10th

I wake to the churn of the bow thrusters.
We are stopped again in the open ocean.
Every sixty kilometres we stall
on dynamic positioning. The ship shudders, motionless
in the most turbulent seas in the world.

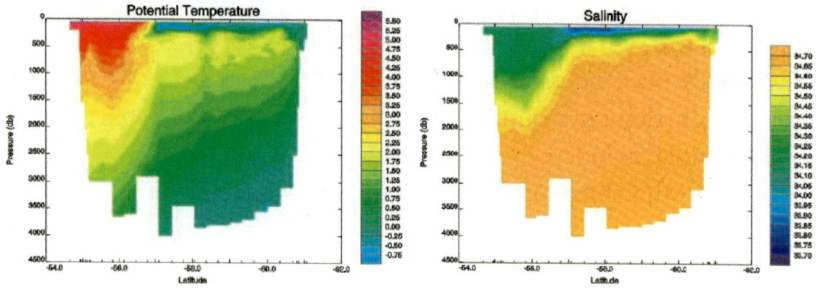

December 11th

He appears somewhere over Burdwood Bank, a single chaperone
outside my cabin porthole and remains for a week.
From time to time he looks at me, turning his head,
and gives me that avian stare: depthless, unreflective
yet knowing. He can do this without losing course;

he doesn't need to look where he is going.
What do you want, I think. Why stick by me?

Near the top of the Peninsula we run out of night.
He stays flying through the diurnal glare.
I wake in my cabin at three in the morning
raise the night shade and there he is,
never flapping his wings. Why won't he give up?
The same old reason: too much history.

Four years later I will meet a true friend who
will tell me the secret of these creatures:
they don't know where
they are going.

December 12th

A sun-bolted conversation
all buoy and butter. His helium smile.

Outside: storm petrels, empty
of censure.

Insomnia is like a summons
(that which comes can
also go). We stay up all night
watching darkness dissolve.

Nightlessness — there will be time enough
for hapless amoral confessions
for red planes to zip into the sinking burning
sky. Time enough
to recall the names

of all the people you never
much liked.

There will only be time.

December 13th

Scientist 19

The threat of night and wine. The scientist at work
in her cabin. Instead of cataloguing
salinity she reads a poem about the prelude
to war, about shields that snag on blood hooks, spears
that hanker for sinew. Most things, she realises,
are like this: waiting for data, conclusions.
Waiting to be proved wrong. Between mealtimes
she performs idle calculations about
variability in the path of the current,
luminescence, chances not taken, the exact
calibration between fear and caution. Outside
her porthole night slides by. An albatross
skims the ship. The Drake Passage breathes some
dark news about an adamant cold flame,
about how a space must be maintained,
in order for all this not to end.

Glacier, 11pm

A congealed abyss
more sublime
than crystals

Who does not want to merge
with a fabulous angel?

This is the meaning of the term, *angelus*:
a messenger, transmitting
between the known and the unknown

The hunger
to make a claim
to say
mine and *mine* and *mine*.

You are
a hoax. A dark rebuff
in this denuded Eden
an urn of darkness.

There is nothing to breathe
but your face.

Moss hours. Our
confessions –

Ice Observations

April 17, 1am

Pressure
fast and ruddered. Noise like
heavy surf.

Stern shallows. Floe
shadows. Heavy strain.

Riggings weakened.

May 5, 3.30pm

Sea curdled with knowledge
breaking up
heavings loom astern. Chains
snapping like wires. Clapped-out
tackles.

Anchors disappeared.

May 24, 11.44pm

Old ice fast
then breaking up
dark water-sky, indigo –

a mirage. A shimmering
humid city.

Frost smoke, thin angora
mist.

We never see the moon.

May 28, 3.30am

Moderate gale
increasing to blizzard.

Hauled wires tight.
Creak and groan of
timber.

What is it I am trying
to forget?

This is where I live now
speared by cold fire.

Listing to starboard

new ice
forming.

June 2, 5pm

Ice wind-driven
to south-west.

Moon up, young
and eager.

Rudderless and drifting.

July 8, 2am

We hope we are strong enough
to take the pressure.

Hoisted and cut
hove to.

The strain of distance –

I

July 16, 4.30pm

Who can release us?

Desert maul and cleaving.
our memories hauled away.

Fresh rime on instruments.

Unable to get a bearing.
we need to
break this drift
before winter.

August 9, 2pm

Lethargy lives in the
lunar night

Here we breathe without expectation
fracture and liberation
of a cantilever dream

Creep fatigue
meltwater salvation or

turquoise sastrugi.

Ravines
also a terrane
the barren prism sky.

Radiant shower of
meteors.

We take from life what we
bring to it.

Caught in this
nocturnal cold
gyre

Who can bear us back
to our latitude
of error?

Running out of Night

brash ice

Floating ice rubble. Originates from sea-ice that is breaking up or commonly as debris from calving ice bergs or ice bergs that break up as part of their ongoing erosion. The wreckage of other forms of ice.

●

I don't know the precise point at which night disappeared. Somewhere at the bottom of the Drake Passage, after Elephant Island and the tabular icebergs. The night convergence, the night boundary? All I know is that we went to sleep one night in the sun.

●

After leaving the continent, an iceberg will live for somewhere between three and twelve months. It sets sail, a ship in these underworld waters, drifts crystal and sure, a floating city. Later, I will have many dreams about this: skyscrapers made of ice, frozen cities floating then ramming ashore in the Falkland Islands. But the ice citadels are too big to be absorbed; they destroy the islands.

•

The light falls so thick it offers cover in its exposure, a glaring shelter. He says, *I think sleeping is a waste of time.* I have to agree. I have nearly stopped sleeping myself and wonder if this is what they call Big Eye – insomnia triggered by 24 hour daylight.

Every morning I fall awake, up and up.

To astound: what does this mean? To knock you out. A sickening.

•

The horizon gets no closer.

In my cabin I have tacked up maps and cards of disintegrating expedition ships, dogs looking on, I think mournfully, though you can't see their faces. Then old bases, snow piling outside.

Chunks of white, loaves gone wrong. They appear when we are just inside the Antarctic Convergence, like sentries. The sudden sting in the air. A light cobalt blue ice underside, filtered and sheared.

pressure ice

Ice having any readily observed roughness of the surface. Ice that has a history of disturbed growth and development.

The sea here is black, asphalt black. I don't know if this is because everything else is white, or if the water reflects the charcoal volcanic rock of the mountains. Even when the sun is out, the sea looks like molten tar.

•

For another six weeks there will be no night. Here's the skua, bearing down on me like a miniature pterodactyl, its thug beak, saurian eye. I feel his absence among the radio antennae and slug seals. His magnetism, who is he exerting it upon even now as I think of him, stranded with the seals and the zinging signals?

Rose and shadows; a summer night in the iron islands. Elephant Island, Clarence Island. There on a narrow beach men survived in upturned boats. They learned that there is the common world and the dreaming world. In the dreaming world they ate mutton chops with mint sauce. In the common world they were lost.

•

All night it is dawn and by five in the morning the light is a noon sun. Lava sky, night burning to the west, an unbroken sea to New Zealand. Ice stills the sea, steady as an oil slick close to the coast, sea ice bunching. The landscape changes here each day, lagoons become choked with ice, icebergs appear at the end of the runway. Yes there is something radical in this place. Also irrational. I pore over an Ice Atlas, a map of the seasonal ice extent caused by the Antarctic polar front. The continent is locked in; in winter, it doubles its mass. You can't get here at all.

névé

Loose granular ice in transition from snow to glacier ice.

Ice is a solitary material. It is like time flowing into outlets, blockages, concentrically and slow. Ice does not give, but takes. The iceberg passes us, like some monumentally stern town. It is smaller now, rotted by heat. Scalloped and porous, it has arches, porticos, columns, rifts. It is dying.

●

He told me that more and more icebergs are calving from the glaciers. They retain their crevasses: we can see them, their deep cobalt veins, although we usually steer clear. They are mostly beneath the surface; I imagine their roots, a tree branching out in all directions, seeking shipwreck.

The ice heart. It is naked, unadorned, a cold cathedral, like the berg we saw last night.

I come from a lean town. I am not used to being in a land this cold and for there to be no wolves.

Now the iron currents flow but in two months they'll be paralysed by ice, caught in a parable, frozen for half a year.

●

Now we live in a sunlit present tense, released from memory. I miss the orange-burn nights of the city, the velvet dark. I know now I can survive without the cover of darkness. I know now that night is not necessary. For months I had no shadow; the Antarctic sun stalls overhead. Only in Februrary does our shadow return, and we flinch in surprise.

stamuhka

A single fragment of ice stranded on a shoal.

Once beyond the pack, bergs risk disintegration. In the open sea, their days are numbered. Even the largest tabular bergs we see will be brash within months. Colossal at the beginning, lakes form on their tops, pools of meltwater. In the dusk which disappeared before the floodlit nights we travel through now, they looked ominous, like envoys or oracles. We were sure they had some message, that we had to take heed.

•

Ice doesn't need us. You can't survive on it. It knows itself, it is older than us, better than us. I look at the calendars people have tacked up in their offices: *Wild Wales 2006* – green fields, leaves breathing, lightning fluvial places. There is no rain here, no electrical activity. I miss the hasty skies of England. This seems to me a place you come to in order to find out, finally, what it is you value.

Why do these icebergs leave? What is their reckless quest? They will only die.

The sun shines, but it seems to swallow itself whole. The icefield is a mirror; we see its imprint on the sky.

rotten ice

Old ice which has become honeycombed in the course of melting and which is in an advanced stage of disintegration.

What we fear most in the Antarctic is fire. Fire on the ship, fire on the base. Fires here are uncontainable. Everything is dry, a spark can start them. We rub and rub against each other until we are frayed. You can't light candles, we are denied their consolation.

•

Night has returned now, its vervet fur. To the south, near the Pine Island glacier, the ice is fastening up. Soon its scrawl will interlock, rebuff the sun once more. I will write this back in the north, in the season of the sun, his season. Darkness tilts toward us again, and he does not lean on its outer rim as he did last year, unknown. The winter is vicious, it is uninhabitable, I see that now. Everything has fled: seals, skuas, petrels. In their wake is written: *time to go*.

This is how it should be: there should be a cadre of people moving through the world who are completely oblivious to the pain and distress of the people who love them. There are the givers and the takers, two apparent tribes.

•

Another ship. Leaving the continent now, months later, in winter. In the Antarctic only later in winter does the sea-ice congeal, buckle its grip upon the continent. The ice shelf lurks somewhere around Pine Island Bay, building, building. Night has galloped toward us; this past month we lost half an hour's light every day. Night rammed back into us some time in late February and it was like encountering the pelt of a giant animal, something purring and thick with waiting.

These are the facts of the world as we know it: that it began in fire, and that it has known periods of ice, and that the ice is going away. We will live on a winterless planet. He is back in his office now, constructing the ice sheets of the distant past; he can tell the future by plotting the past. These are the facts.

•

We are on a rough mission. It's too easy to claim solitude, deprivation, to imagine we have been transformed. The light is transparent, electric. We rock the ship, it sallies from side to side trying to dislodge the ice. We are stuck.

For the first time I lock my cabin door. Scientist 19 has locked herself away. Night is on retreat. Soon we will not be able to settle into the skin of oblivion. We have been too long away, or not enough. That point in the journey where it is either one or the other but it is not clear which.

We are only floating on the earth's crust, itself at sea on a layer called the aesthenosphere. We are fugitives, we are on the moon. We cannot walk on the ice, we would die. We cannot swim in the water, we would die. We can wait the ice to shift, to break up.

•

I have become a believer in facts. I believe in his helium smile, I believe that the sun is a God which bestows its favour upon us brutally, even in the plastic ribbed mats which keep the plates from sliding to the floor, the shocks we get each time we touch metal on the ship. How that current which moves between us and links us has nothing to do with any other human experience. How in the end it is a different energy to everything else human. Which do we choose, fire or ice? Is it even possible to know, in a day that lasts three months? Night is coming now, arcing toward us on the planet that tilts 23.5 degrees, listing like a broken ship.

•

The night is an old code, 'a moment of wrench and unrest'. Desire, I remember, requires imagination. Also ignition.

How to discard grief? Walk away lighter.

Night Flight, March 5th

Missing a friend is not the same as missing a lover.
We are waiting for the return of the Dash 7
back from Stanley for the last time. He went
and is flying back the same day because tomorrow
Horace the computer weather model says
it will close in. Soon the pilots will leave for the winter
taking the planes with them. Leaving the Antarctic
is like leaving no other place on earth. You go back
not to a place but to another dimension.
There, time is not a resinous block. You have choices –
what to have for dinner, which of the twenty
shampoos in the supermarket to buy. I stand
on the veranda with Darren, a Saint –
one of the domestics from St Helena.
He is smoking because he's homesick. We wait
for the lights to appear in the sky over
Jenny Island, for the return of our envoy
to the world of cash and keys and mobile phones.
Perhaps he can tell us what has changed. Here night
is still new to us. For a long time we slept
in day. Now it is the dark which wakes us
at four in the morning, a reverse insomnia.
It's six-thirty and already dusk. The runway lights are lit
for the last time this season. Darren and I wait,
bundled in our fleeces. We try not to think about how

a void swirls at the centre of things. The Dash appears
first as two sparks under a black sky. Its nickname
is 'the air tractor'; it flies almost slow enough to hover.
To miss a friend is not the same as to miss a lover.
But tonight the plane's return feels like a saviour.
It feels like he has been gone forever.

NOTEBOOK: MARCH 14, 2006

The world is hardening. In the bay this process starts as ice flowers, tiny crystalline formations. As the carpet of flowers is knit together by cold nights they are soaked by seawater to form a grey gruel; overnight, as the temperature plummets, the gruel becomes porridge. Within days pancake ice, a dusky ivory, forms. These frozen waterlillies float on the suddenly placid surface of a thickening sea, their edges ridged upward where they have rubbed against one another. S. our summer base commander, who wintered here two years ago, tells me that when these ridges start to glue together, 'that's when you can say the sea ice has begun to form. That's the beginning of winter.'

The Antarctic Convergence

uncharted waters

Sleeking through
dead men names: Brabant, Livingston, Biscoe
the Graham Coast. Sixteen knots
in uncharted waters.

To the west, the Bellingshausen
Abyssal plain, the Charcot
Deep-Sea Fan.

Names here are less lunar
than places you might
fight an unwinnable war: the Sentinel Range
The Heritage Mountains.

Names borrowed
from the expired rapture
of long-departed boots:
Doake Ice Rumples, Dufek Massif

Two favourites: Whichhaway Nunataks
The Executive Committee Range.

Soon we will stand
where no others have. I never hoped
to be the first at anything, or anywhere

All night we will pick our way
between reefs and islets
on radar, charts, instinct. Tonight

the Master will not sleep.

magnetic poles

A wandering magnetism.
The spike and guile of him.

The south magnetic pole is where the earth's
magnetic fields are vertically aligned.
The pole can move very rapidly,
sometimes hundreds of kilometers a day.
Sometimes it's not in the Antarctic at all
but a hundred kilometres
out in the ocean.

He tells me the planet's alignment is changing
energy fields will be turned inside out.

The last time this happened on earth
humans didn't exist. Whales and birds
and eels will lose their bearings, their
migrations stalling.

We will all be southerners then.

new years' eve

In the RIB
we wind among ice floes
bump through a sea of transparent ice.

We haul a chunk into the boat
this will be the bartender's stock
for New Years' Eve.

We will drink G&Ts made with remnants
of glaciers. We cut the motor and float through
ice gruel, the grate of it against
the propeller.

Penguins hoot. Otherwise, silence.

on characters

G. the carpenter, he speaks like a child, low, long nearly slurred vowels. He is 'the glue of the base' apparently. There are many flat vowels here as it happens, the steamrollered 'o's and 'a's of D., the Northern Irish weather forecaster. The cook is mean or indifferent, it doesn't matter which. Desire flourishes here, apparently, although not necessarily of the serious kind. *What happens on base stays on base.* They think they can keep it in separate compartments but we are connected. By satellite I can ring my friend on his mobile in London and there he is in Soho, going to a film. Some of them try too hard, like the plumber, who touts himself as the base eccentric. Shreds of intent, the sky drizzles snow. Inside men wear shorts and hiking socks in Teva sandals. The Canadian air mechanic wears a kilt, bare legs, Teva sandals and a Mohawk haircut. The sun like kleig lights, it falls down straight with no warning, a gold axe.

leopard seal

The cat-seal is watchful, carniverous.
The mottled steel of its back.
She was snorkeling. Everyone remembers
she was in love with this place.

It happened in winter. A plane came
all the way from Canada
to take her body home.

They tell me the shock hung
over the base, reverberated
well into the following summer.

We see them in the bay
their sleek charcoal fur,
their thin leering mouths.

the convergence zone

Three masses of water
make up the ocean
below 55 degrees South:
Antarctic Surface Water
Circumpolar Deep Water
Antarctic Bottom Water.

Cold surface water moving north
away from Antarctica meets warmer
water moving south
both circling continent

at four times the speed of the
Gulf Stream. A separation as effective
as any wall or boundary
the border of nobody's country.

the ordinary year

Sidereal time, ephemeris time, mean solar days, Zulu Time. I learn that the sidereal year is the time it takes the earth to make one complete orbit of the sun – 365.25636 days, a little longer than the ordinary solar year. Its official name is that: the Ordinary Year. No ordinary year, this. Suddenly I am on a loop. A winter childhood: snow, trailers, formica. Trailing behind other peoples' existences. Linoleum on the walls, shotguns in the bedroom, cars that won't start. Coming at the base from the back end of the Point – radio transmitters emitting radiation, gigantic Julian the man-mountain driving around in a Gator. Piles of rubble, drums, boxes, corrugated iron arch sheds, all strung between tower lines like a cross between a granite quarry and a penal colony. But then you walk around the Point and the base disappears and you hear only the groan and rustle of icebergs melting, a wide ring of mountains, and you are in the Antarctic. Then back to the penal colony after a trip to the Monument, a reminder that people died here, that it is a dangerous place.

salinometer

All night we take measurements
from a device that looks like
an ice cream machine.

He funnels the bottles, I record the numbers.
We are beneath the waterline
technically submerged.

He tells me *Seism* means shock.
that an elastic medium
can be subjected to two types of deformation:
compression and shear.

The language of ice
is one of rent and quiver.
I tell him about other kinds
of stress and flux: *Ludus, Storge, Mania,
Pragma, Eros.* He tells me
P waves and *S* waves are determined
by elastic perameters.

Ice scrapes against the hull.
If we put our hands
on the walls we can feel the ridges
as we grind through.

All night we feel the ice this way
sometimes emerging onto the deck
for air and see the *chien-loup* —
what cinematographers call twilight:
the wolfhound.

The mountains are wolfish too
winter cousins in storm cloaks.
We glide through
a rose-grey perpetual dusk.

Our shift ends at breakfast
we climb up above deck
for coffee.

the antithesis

The north rests
under the constellation
the Greeks called *Arktos*.
Its opposite is *Antarkitkos*.

Poor place
with no name of its own
only somewhere it's not.

the tagging board

These are the places we can be:

On Base, Flying, Off Base,
Runway, Bonner Lab
Vals, Boat House
Around the Point

the field assistant
nearly died 300 metres from our front door

slipped down an ice cliff
slid onto an ice shelf

could have tried to swim
but you won't last five minutes in this water

he forgot to tag out
so he wasn't found until morning
alive

clever staircases
of salvation

winding up and down.

thresholds

They talk about hope here about
having a durable heart
but ignition is forbdiden
because we fear fire.

The creatures in the aquarium
are being probed for the upper
temperature threshold
of their survivability.

They are burning too
but slowly. As Shackleton said
we are reduced to 'the naked soul of man'.

But rather than succumb to despair
we grow and grow
giants of the plateau
our hearts exploding.

Ice Diaries

1. The ship

A cocktail party on the bridge the night
before we sail south. Men in indigo uniforms
slide through the blue night, the summer sun
a low red flush. Navigation screens show the track
we will follow, the weather systems that lie in wait.
We love the science fiction names for the places
on the ship, the Rough Workshop, the Cool
Specimen Room, the Transducer Space.
We are on a mission to map oblivion.
We will cross the Antarctic Circumpolar current –
the only current to flow around the globe
without encountering any land barrier.
For now our world is this ship. It is like being
a family: we eat together, sleep
in adjoining beds, hold vagrant conversations.
We are at the mercy of proximity.
He appears in my cabin door, says
without introduction or greeting:
*There are two things that might possibly
interest you – real coffee and boardgames.*
Just north of Burdwood Bank we go up
to Monkey Island to stargaze. The Seven Sisters
fade in and out of view on the eastern horizon
strobe-lit, electric. Orion is reversed,
his sword points north. The seismic ship –
off to blow up the seabed in search of natural gas –

glitters on the black lacquer of the ocean.
I struggle to catalogue this feeling: is it
to not quite be able to believe your luck?
An amnesty from doubt? Later
we will play Scrabble, drink wine as the ship
begins to grapple with the Drake Passage.

He is studying the dynamics of ice.
He likes explanations. He moves through space
as if he owns it. To me,
he confesses uncertainties.

Messages brew in the dark.
Something of the mystery and wonder
of the world has been re-introduced
to me, after a long period of corrosion.

The physicist with us, he says it is a problem of scale.
The human mind staggers
at the notion of an atom.

'We haven't got a feeling of what happens
at that scale, at the subatomic level,' he says.
'We have no intuition.'

The sun streams through my cabin window at 8.24pm, a perpetual setting sun. In a few minutes I will go up to the bridge and see the brass, vermilion, the brash peach of roses.

G. the biologist says: 'what happens on the ship stays on the ship'.
S. the deck engineer, met his wife on board. She was a scientist. 'Well',
he says. 'It happens'.

10.40pm. Clouds leer, scattered to a blood horizon. We are still again
in the middle of the Passage, doing a station. The CTD is lowered to
2500 metres, its deepest point.

•

We watch storm petrels skirt the waves, buoyed
on updraft. At night we sail through snowstorms.
Flurries come at us like fireworks thrown up from a void.

Night begins to thin until it is a sleek animal.
On one of these fading nights we see our first tabular berg
at 2am from the UIC lab. It is busy, self-important.
It is five kilometeres long. In three months,
the oceanographer says it will be gone.

•

The whiteness has wiped out my dreams. All I have now
is raw experience: I eat, drink, play games
of Scrabble in the Officer's Bar.
Things which demand to be understood
without interpretation:

I already know I will have to live without him
but am delaying the thought.
His invitations to intimacy come wrapped
in an instinct to hurt. These are easily confused, of course.

To defend myself I try to organise my thoughts
into meaningful categories, some schema
of understanding. This is what I write:

1. *The Wrecks*
2. *Projects which have their roots in periods of despair*
3. *Trying to Stay Light*
4. *An Encyclopedia of the Night*

●

We thread through glaciers, ice tongues, terranes,
through ice-streams, and anchor in the defunct crater
of Deception Island. We deploy sediment traps,
moorings, gather what we can about the life of krill.
Then slope down the peninsula; in four days we will arrive
on a gravel spit the other side of Adelaide Island.

Frozen night-mornings we are up on Monkey Island.
He catalogues the ice for me – *frazil ice,
frost flowers, stamhuka* – seeing in the flesh
what for him is usually a computer model, and it is
just that: flesh. Its folds and wrinkles, its
overlapping tongues of skin. It calves, and carves.

We sleek through it, the bow scalps our channel.
Beyond the glacier valley the pack awaits.

●

Two days later we are stuck. Pack ice
travels in thug groups, it seethes with seals.

The Master tells us we can be stopped for weeks

if we are unlucky. I want nothing more than this:
for us to be marooned together in this stalled rapture.

•

Scrubbed sunset. Shadowed sockets of drifting pack ice, the stars themselves run from its distrust. Dawn is not dawn but an oyster light painted at a skimming angle, the Antarctic night a lowering blue vein on snow. Snow reflects a white censor sun flooding the bridge. Now we know everything we need to know about vastness and impossible scales. This upheaval. The brawl of ice.

•

He is a ripe sun, not bleached
like the true polar sun. He is a fire in the mind.
This is how I will know him, the ellipsis
searing the sky.
An iceberg's life-cycle is about decay. The minute it is born
it begins to die.

We are
seekers of pain. Survivors. An old story.

2. Blind lead[1]

There is no mother but that dark
centre. Shoals of winter trees.

Those years of my life
are like a funnel.

A tundra of selves.

I learned about scorn there.
About how difficult it might be
to distinguish freezing
from scorching.

●

I remember being put out on the veranda to sleep in minus 30 degrees. This was a tradition, to toughen up infants. There was an absence-shaped person who was lost, that was all I knew. For seven months of the year it was winter, a devastation of stasis visited upon the land, scriptural in its brutality. Soot clouds like coal-smoke snaked across the sky. I thought: all living things are dead, only we are alive. The flow and fabric of time seemed as one – there was no frontier, no threshold. We dissolved into winter.

---

[1] A lead through the ice with only one outlet, ie a cul-de-sac

3. Deep field[2]

A gleam of albedo, then sudden dusk – the chrome edge
of a blizzard. We hunker down; suddenly our world
has that sound: *hunkering* – a search for lean comfort,
also a resignation. We abandon our tent
and lay out P-bags in the back of the Otter.
I wait for the tent to be blown away, a shred
which will rise, whipped into a birdless sky.

The mountains scowl, then are draped in white.
We dig out the meths, get the Primus going.
Gas screams through the ring. We must decide who will go out
get snow to melt, stake the pee flag. Storm-night comes.
It is day but dark. The pilot says:
they didn't see this one coming, did they?

The plane, blanked down, sways in the wind.
The Tilley Lamps we hang from the ceiling warm us
until we crawl out of sleeping bags.
The pyramid tent is anchored with snow
piled on its valences. But overnight the snow has shifted.
I have to go out to re-secure it, before it blows away.
The pilot says, not without a lifeline. But we are
only sixty feet away. You ever been in a whiteout?
This is one. He clips a wire around my belt.

Outside the plane, the air is a prism.
It has levels: cold, ice, the tear and scrape
of wind, but also just that: cold. Snow-stumble,

---

[2] In the Antarctic, a science camp far from base

a creak and grind. The snow is coarse, grainy,
it smothers footsteps. Then the tent disappears.
I fumble for the wire, tug it. The pilot
tugs back. I catch a ribbon of shout, imagine
you still there? We can no longer see each other.

Too late for the spiral of explanations.
I am bent by the wind by fiery quartz spears.
The mind staggers against the facts: we want to know
the principles by which matter functions.

We are living each moment as a part of itself,
like holograms which if you dissect them,
turn out to be only a perfect copy of the whole.
I repent. I will work now with the grain of life.
I want to know its purpose, its laws. The snow
slouches into the Otter behind me like a stray dog.

•

For the next two days the Otter is our rescue,
we burrow into P-bags, console ourselves
with cognac stashed in the cockpit. What is the name
of this freedom? To seek shelter, to eat and sleep
in the very machine that will vault us into the sky.

No, we do not become lovers. But his power
is seductive: we are the only humans
for two thousand miles in every direction,
and only he knows how to get us out of here.
Otherwise, we are corpses. Other people's guilt.

•

Indigo seas swallow our albedo: the amount of light
we reflect back into the cosmos.
These shoreless seas sizzle with melt. All around
tar water brews gigantic fish.
Even the plane – vermilion, ecstatic – pales.

We talk about the past: the things we have done
or wish we had done. But this is no place
for the low famine of regret.
In our blank hours we feed on the fiction
of ourselves, concoct overlapping stories,
repeat anecdotes. Anything to drown out
the roar of silence.

●

In everyday life there is too much colour, trivia, analysis.
I want it to be simple again, reduced. Days of captivity
of four-hour games of pocket Scrabble. Mad days
connected to each other by a wire. So that if I tugged,
he would feel me.

●

The storm retracts its claws and we take off
into a chrome sun. Four hours' flying
and we are back on base where we are served mince pies:
Home for tea and medals.

Down in our Ellsworth camp I thought a lot
about other places I could be. But how less
knotted with desire. Bleached days
fed on waiting, some sky mire fallen on us. That distant sun
in a shroud of ice crystals.

Later, I will wonder, what was the magic?
He is not my lover, but those days spent together
in the fuselage, waiting for the storm to pass
idly making up our Ideal Restaurant Meals
will feel not like time that needed to be passed.
We were settled in no-one's country, and it, ownerless,
gave us in return its fierce vacant squalor.

4. Ablation[3]

The end of summer is a melt carnival
rivulets and streams course under the ice,
frost smoke shrouds the horizon. Around the Point

seals calve and loll in mint-jelly patches of algae,
brown smears of uterus blood. The penguins moult
unhappily – their feathers create too much drag
and they are vulnerable to predators –
leopard seals and their snake mouths, orcas
with their whining cry, their beachball eyes.

The sun is floodlit, immense. We have no shadows.
I cannot really remember night, its solitude, its disguise.

Here it is warming faster than anywhere on earth.
There are days when we ski in shorts and t-shirts.

One day the world will be ice-less, we will be
released from winter. Winter:
it is there in the word, the hollow ring
of absence. Days passed unnoticed by anyone you love.
Days without spirit or hunger.

[3] The disappearance of an ice or snow surface by melting and/or evaporation.

•

Love, like hope, does not melt
or otherwise go away. It remains, wind-carved
an empty statue to its former gleam.

People speak of burying it, like a corpse.
It is like death in that respect:
you have no choice but to accept its loss,
that we are in the maw of some powerful thing
and all we have is the conviction of our desires.

We are only every howling hunger
artist, busy with lust. Ice has made us
what we are. I just wanted to be taught
by you, to talk to you about the properties
of these blasted carnal fissures
we call selves.

Hawk noons drill straight through us.
We have punctured this magnetic orb.

There is skin, and stone and bone here –
because we loved here, once

this was our home.

5. Winter

We leave the continent in April
already winter with its stripped winds.
The days are still light although the sun flirts
with the horizon in the lava sky
of a disowned summer.

The ship thrusts away from the wharf where
the winterers hold old flares aloft,
a livid burn in the darkness.

On the horizon the prowl and yaw
of white-sprung mountains: knives which split us
into new and better selves.

The moment is erosion. Epic floes sweep
north, leaving the continent now
for the vertigo of tomorrow.

Endurance

We call the ship that has come to pluck us out
our big red taxi. Its real name is the *Endurance*
a namesake of Shackleton's
broken vessel.

It is April. Leaving Antarctica in winter
is like slouching away from a doomed village:
tidepools now clogged with ice,
a gorged sky. Time passes like saints
watching their backs.

The horizon is a blue strip of light
between ice and sea, cloud and mountain.

We live like liar peasants.
The air only hooks. Struck dumb to find
we are enemies of ourselves
in an obsessive present.

We used to know so many things.
Now we are strung on
one thin rule:

not far now
until the darkness.

ARCTIC

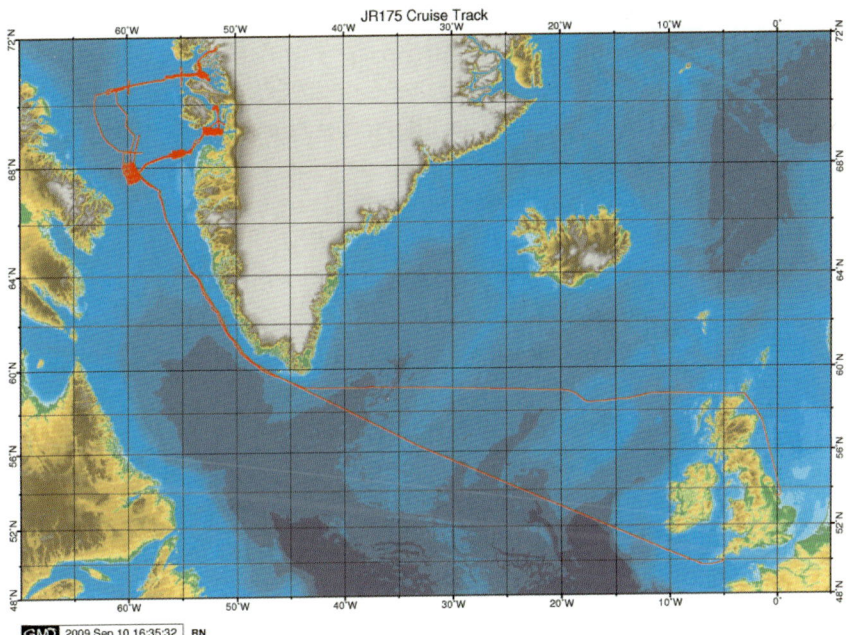

NOTEBOOK – AUGUST 15TH, 2009

Mid-Atlantic, somewhere south of Iceland

The Arctic point of no return passed in September 2007, when the summer sea ice extent in the region was at its lowest in recorded history. In Alaska, indigenous people say 'the earth is faster.' In Siberia they say 'gone is the bowl of winter.' The bowl used to have depth and bite – those long weeks in January and February when bitter temperatures reigned. Now the bowl is a plate. From its edges slips the land's memory of deep cold.

All over the Arctic the seasons come sooner, the weather changes more quickly and is more volatile. It is as if the pulse of the planet itself is quickening.

Although it has a major role to play in global warming, the glacial past of Greenland, and in particular of its coastal waters, has been surprisingly little investigated. Most of the money and attention has gone to the Antarctic. Our goal is to study the behaviour of a major ice stream in Greenland in the Late Quaternary – the last few hundred thousand years. To do this we will be running the ship over the seabed where this ice stream is thought to have once exited, as well as sidling up to the Jakobshaven Isbrae, the fastest-flowing ice stream in the world.

Two Sunrises

'Two sunrises, 0538 and 0547, through a cleft and then over the mountains as we moved, loads of bergs, and a light to behold.'

Blackwater and oval, bittersweet musk of morning. Two sunrises and we are doubly alive. Suddenly origin and destiny are the same. We enter Igdlorssuit Sund. September and the planet hesitates on its axis before diving into autumn. Kangigdleq – the centre pulls us in. Everything there is to know about life is in the light on the water, its rebel arc unmatched by these severe capes. At the mouth of Karrat Isfjord a tongue of ice lolls, called Rinks Isbrae. Crushed to grow so at home here, stalled lovers of summer.

Letter to the Shadow Man

In a documentary last night, the Icelandic
photographer captured a Greenlandic woman
eating a raw bird. *I see a man in the shadows,
watching you. He does not like you, this man.*
I watched as the hunters flensed skin from seal
and bear blubber and thought: adipose, toxins –
then the glistening white bear with the tobacco
muzzle, hounded to death by the hunters' dogs.
Although first he knocks one unconscious.
They are very clever animals, the old hunter
tells me. Smart enough to have dreams.
All night I dreamt of freezing barbecues in Iceland,
all of us eating in our salopettes.
He is angry with you, has been for centuries.
Both of us have forgotten why, or over what.
*For him there is no remedy. He will take
away the good things that are coming.*
Dire prophecies encourage extreme rational thinking:
if he takes them away, can they be said to be coming?
Perhaps cancelled is the better word. On this trip
I've outwitted the shadow man, left him
standing on the pier. Then who is that man
in his sombre suit on the jetty in Ilulissat?
The curator of the ice sculpture garden, perhaps.
The hunters here are no cleverer than the ice bear,
they just have dogs. I can't stomach it here –
too much blubber, too much fate. 'I love
my country,' says the hunter back from the ice.

'It can let me live, or it can kill me. Today
it let me live.' The idea is that the shadow man
disports himself at my distress. He lets me live
so that he can feed from my pain. Here I think
of deserts, of caution, of my own failings.
The hunters used to spend a month on the ice.
Now its fissures drive them to shore within a week.
Here, the hunters say, there are no degrees of
survival: you either stay alive or you don't:
'what you people call luck is really the intentions
of the spirits.' They are always around us,
coming to decisions, calculating distress
on their choirs of abacuses. I can't take it
anymore, I tell them. But they know I can. They know
I will simply go on. So, shadow man,
these men with the stone faces tell me
it is bad luck to acknowledge your existence,
let alone talk to you. But here goes:
we are alive today, our country did not kill us.
See our triumph as we gnaw the starling,
its heart still fluttering.

NOTEBOOK – AUGUST 20TH, 2009

We swath by day for safety in these largely unsurveyed waters, because we need the visibility to keep the ship on its predetermined lines, and core by night, the ship held still on DP in the diluted indigo. At 71 degrees north, according to the GPS, the sun sets at 22.36 and rises at 04.16, but actually it merely skirts the horizon. The angle of the sun, the sea and the presence of ice collude to produce compelling visual effects: the setting sun is black, oval; mirages morph on the horizon – boots, convents, oil rigs. In these waters we are almost alone. Occasionally the MV *Bergen*, a seismic exploration ship – prospecting for oil, probably – comes into view, or we glimpse the Royal Arctic Line ferry, which supplies many of the coastal communities in Greenland, dashing into port. I take to watching the odd transatlantic plane streak through empty skies with binoculars. We are now above the Arctic Circle and well into polar waters. Terns and fulmars skim the black viscous surface, their reflections mirrored in the waves.

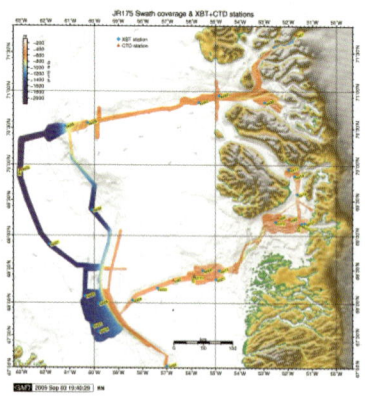

Night Orders
RRS James Clark Ross, Voyage 18

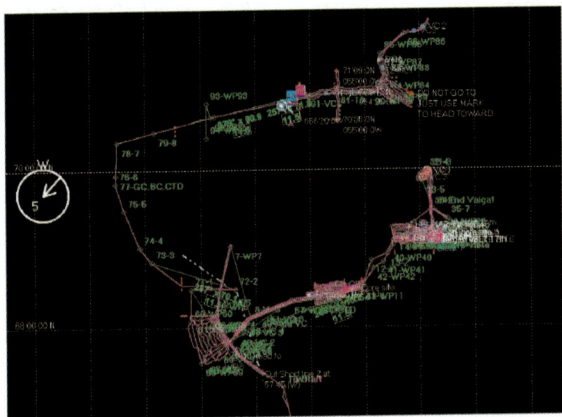

Call me if visibility draws in to less than 2 miles.
Otherwise call me if required, or if in any doubt whatsoever

Somewhere over the Porcupine Abyssal Plain
we gather in the Officer and Scientists' Bar
to hear the Master's story, blackout shades lowered
to remove reflection to the bridge as we slew through
the Atlantic. One of the secret tricks of living,
he tells us, is learning to accept what is written.
So to the Master's Night Orders. He will
tell us the names of necessary accidents,
the coordinates of salvation, how to read
the darkness, because the coast is long.

•

'We were working among high concentrations
of very hard ice of land and sea origin.
Pursued into the channel and running out into
the basin – all those place-names about betrayal
or despair: Deception Island, Exasperation
Inlet. Then the ice sheet collapsed and we took the ship
onto a glacier! It was no longer there, of course,
but still on the charts. Since Larsen B it runs
as a frozen seam into the sea. We were
so capable then. We knew what we loved.'

As dark encroaches, reduce power to make good 10.0kts through the water.
Pass at least 1'.0nm off bergs during darkness, 0'.6nm during daylight.
Call me if required, or if in any doubt whatsoever

Going up on the bridge at night we are
temporarily blinded, passing through
a velvet curtain into a field of black so
absolute people often crash into the pillar.
Then the eye adjusts to a greyscale world,
emerging from it, bursts of luminescence –
spray, the ship pitching into a tar sea trimmed
by phosphorescence. Nothing but open ocean
yet we imagine obstacles, nearly
trigger evasions. At sea, nothing is more real
than ourselves – the whale, the narwhal,
the fulmar are projections, perhaps,
beyond the edge of vision. Each night
we gain time; our clocks are *retarded*
(not *put back*) as we slink across lonely
time zones inhabited only by

mid-Atlantic volcanoes. We will arrive
in Greenland three hours younger.

*Steer TMG 293°T. Remember Clocks and Telephone System to be retarded
One Hour to GMT-1H.
Call me if required, or if in any doubt whatsoever*

'We were in the Amundsen Sea to study
floating tongues of ice where land-bound glaciers
meet the sea. We sent the Autosub3 down under
the shelf. It was melting, sure – warm water everywhere!
No-one knew it was being eroded from within. Then
we moved on to the Getz Ice Shelf. At home, away
from this life, we enter a puzzle of emptiness
no longer connected to the decaying fire.'

*Use the forward searchlight during the hours of darkness
Call me if required, or if in any doubt whatsoever*

At night we follow a stricter course, the past
in front of us, the future behind.
On the bridge a navigation lamp casts
a bronze pool of light onto the Admiralty
Chart, the compass rose, parallel rule, the
Night Orders book. We are shipping spray over
the foc'sle with every fourth wave; waves
come in sequences: the ninth wave is the
largest, the one that comes flying white
out of the darkness, a foaming flock of birds.

Be aware AT ALL TIMES of the depth and trend of the seabed
Call me if required, or if in any doubt whatsoever

'I skated around Leskov Island in the dark, running
along the 1000 metre contour of the volcano, then
the close-in survey, the island a black mass
amid the darkness on the beam, searchlights on
for growlers lurking in the white horses.
The only noise the echo sounder as the depths
climbed and fell away again, spinning off
the spiral track into deeper waters.

We might move through the world like this, perhaps –
on invisible ships, grouped together not by chance
but by fate. Bubbles whose perimeters
we cannot detect, never mind measure.

One of the horrors of working a ship
over a gas field is that should seabed gas
escape, the bubble would engulf the ship
before you knew what had happened. By the time
we might regain buoyancy it would already
have fallen beneath the waves to 50 metres
below, and so would be crushed and inundated.'

If you encounter pack ice do not enter, but skirt the pack by veering offshore as necessary

Bad weather brings conviviality. We huddle
in the bar, clutching pint glasses with both hands.
We pass over underwater arroyos, the
Iceland Basin, Reykjanes Ridge.

At dawn we return to the bridge to gaze
at the Rothko painting outside the window
one of his funereal canvases in black
and charcoal. The night is graphite, we are
balanced on its meniscus, crushed between sky
and sea, two flatland horizons.
Before we'd crossed it this way, did we believe
the Atlantic existed, or did we think
of it as filler between continents?

At dawn the sea is colder now: pale and
suet-thick. Still no sign of coast.
The strain of distance. Who knows where
we are going?

Call me if required, or if in any doubt whatsoever

69° North

There is a vein of night,
we existed there, trading jade talk around
the world.

Our sleepless republic, its partisan futures
and the almond sky.

Milk and chervil lope on a far coast;
we existed there too, though separated
by waves.

They were amulet days, days we thought could
show us how to die.

The horizon yoked and sober in the sky.

Nansen

As a boy he has a dog named 'Storm'. Years later,
one named 'Flint'. His wife speaks of his 'sweet
reasonableness'. Why then the draw
of the Arctic, its lure of denial? The year
the *Fram* is locked in ice he writes *The Winter Night*,
about the veil of glittering silver that is
the stars, how the polar sky is 'the vault of heaven'.
Between missions he travels to England,
to France, and is perplexed: 'Everyone I saw
was laughing'. He never learns to fail.
He is a 'sturdy, strapping fellow',
so why this penitent heart, the intervals
between exploits that seem only frozen fevers
but turn out to be the real expedition.

Isfjord

'The Kangigdleq, a branch fjord, extends east into the Isbrae. When the glacier calves, the fjord fills completely with ice.'[4]

Ejected from the ship you step onto land and instantly realise your error. The land doesn't move. Girls in singlets and shorts walk down the streets of Ilulissat at 17 degrees. Cue bitter hours when a brassy sun cuts through your mind. Can't move forward can't go back. The heat intense but step outside the sun and cold laps at your edges.

'Kangerdlugssuaq, the S branch of Karrats Fjord, is entered N of Upernivik O (5.33). Qingussaq, an island, fronts the entrance to Kangerdlugssuaq; a chain of islets and rocks.'

There is no way out of the fjord; its mouth is blocked by a tongue of ice. The ice lean and monumental the mind can only understand it through comparison: cathedrals, tors, airliners. Mid-August and the sun only black whalehunter hours in the town warming to its own demise. The sea ice is gone. Here, winter is the real season. Half-feral huskies slink after you through the streets.

'A quantity of explosives were lost (1993) in position 70°40'.5N 52°07'.4W; the explosives were expected to perish over a period of about two years and are not a danger to surface navigation; however until further notice vessels are advised not to fish in the area.'

---

[4] The texts are excerpted from the *British Admiralty Sailing Directions Arctic Pilot* Volume 3 NP12, which covers the Davis Strait and Baffin Bay with the west and north-west coasts of Greenland, the north coast of Canada including Hudson Bay and the Arctic Archipelago. Reprinted by permission.

The ship is nearby. When you mount the crest of a hill on one of your solitary walks you see it in the bay lacquered gold with sun in its stately glide among the bergs. Who could have been so careless with explosives? Things we don't recognise, and dismiss, for appearing in the form we least expect. The ice is refusing to cohere as it once did, now creaky, unstable, the locals say more like slush than ice.

'The known depths in Karrat Isfjord and Kangigdleq are great, about 1100m in places.'

How much energy we receive from the sun is no longer the issue; the organism itself is warming. That gentle pressure is gone, which allows us to exist, an unpartisan bubble. Now minutes become individual palaces of impossibility. Tarnished glint of sun, the dark moss rocks, icebergs on fire, a giddy melt carnival. You will never come this way again.

NOTEBOOK – SEPTEMBER 2ND 2009

Greenlandic Place Names From the Admiralty Charts

Qeqertarssuatsiaq (island)
Kangerdluarssugssuaq (inlet)
Hamborgerland (area)
Sukkertoppen (town)
Kitdliaraq (lighthouse)
Pisugfik (island)
Satsigsuarqat (islets)
Eqalunguit Nunat (island)
Sangmissorssuaq (mountain)
Fiskenaeshumplen (mountain)
Fiskenaesset (town)
Kingigtuarssuk (islets)
Tasiussassuaq (Fjord)
Ravns Storo (isle)
Qaqajungnarssuaq (mountain)
Majorssuit (isles)
Qagssissalik (islet)
Qaqat Nalagat (mountain or lake)
Satuarssugssuaq (light & beacon)
Pingotukut (isle)
Oqutalik (isle)

Arctic Pilot
NP12 Disko Bay – Ilulissat[5]

CHAPTER 4
WEST COAST OF GREENLAND
DISKO BUGT – DISKO ISLAND – VAIGAT

General Information

Ice

'Very large icebergs come in their thousands from fjords on the E side of Disko Bugt and Vaigat, after the winter ice breaks up in May. Many of them enter Davis Strait and Baffin Bay, S of Godhavn (Qeqertarsuaq) and through Vaigat, respectively, to be carried N by the West Greenland Current.'

Who will tell you where to go when you are
on the wrong latitude. These lightning days of summer
only a temperate survey of the heart.
For fourteen days I lived by charts and maps,
echoes and forays. Now shore life seems strange and crass.

---

[5] The texts are excerpted from the *British Admiralty Sailing Directions Arctic Pilot* Volume 3 NP12, which covers the Davis Strait and Baffin Bay with the west and north-west coasts of Greenland, the north coast of Canada including Hudson Bay and the Arctic Archipelago. Reprinted by permission.

In the airport fretting French people – vital
partnerless women in their forties – parade across
the departure lounge in North Face gear. Greenlanders
in scuffed trainers sit clutching plastic bags
tied with string. The morning is stern and cool.
Four weeks ago I was in Athens, a heat like war.

The plane snags on air and we are flying.
From the Dash 7 I can't see the ship,
which has moved off among the bergs to work
in Disko Bay. We fly above the Isbrae,
its mash of bergs thrust from the ice sheet
now wallowing in warming water,
lucent hexagons adrift in brash. Ice
is a slow wave – a frozen process,
but still a process; there is no end, only
a transfer of energy. We bank, turning inland,
and return to summer.

•

Flora

'Of edible berries the crowberry is widely spread; the bilberry or bog whortleberry is less common; the cloudberry or mountain raspberry rarely ripens. Scurvy grass and sorrel are also found.'

The continent sprouts reindeer moss, called
tripe de roche, and saxifrage. The *Pilot* gives
this advice should the mariner ever find himself
wrecked on shore and forced to forage.

I took a warm flapjack from the Duty Mess
which lasted me three days. In the bay
by the town, bonfire sunsets
extinguish themselves in fleeting bergs,
grounded on some unnamed gyre.
A town of plywood basements, of hungry
summering dogs pacing in their chains, floury flies
so gorged on heat they forget to bite. Over sphagnum
moss spattered with smashed beer bottles we walked
to the ice stream, a lithe river of ice
drawling frozen cathedrals into the sea.
On the ship no-one's doors were locked. Days
passed like unordinary wrecks spawning
mirrorgliders – those birds who graze the waves
in search of thrill. There our only vocation
was avoiding disaster. We glided into
Disko Bay glass-calm under hawk skies, the Isbrae's
bergs skimming terns and disintegration
drinking wine on the foc'sle in our shirtsleeves.

●

Tides

'There is a curious local effect called the *Kanele* which is produced, particularly at the time of spring tides, by the calving of large icebergs, or by a discharge of ice from Jakobshavns Isfjord. This causes a regular and heavy swell and, without any warning, a long flat wave up to 2 m in height with a period of about 6 minutes.'

Surges
leap from mind to mind
lying head to toe in cabins, we share dreams.

For four years since I was last on it, I dreamt
of this ship. We would be at sea and
tsunamis were hurtling toward us
which we always vanquished.

Now that I am here the only trauma
is an unearned elation.

Time is a crystal river which slows, congeals,
creates floes. Here, sometimes
we are stranded.

•

Approaches

'Disko Bugt is entered from W between Egedesminde (Aasiaat) (68°43'N 52°53'W) and Godhavn (Qeqertarsuaq), 35 miles NNW. The entrance is encumbered with islands and dangers, but there are deep channels between them. More islands and dangers lie on and in the vicinity of shoal water in the SE part of the bight.'

I can't forget the way the drunk teacher
pronounced 'Sisimuit'. She came to smoke
next to the icebergs and the huskies
in the Arctic hotel in Ilulissat.
She had green eyes and a moustache.
The word like the hissing of water on hot stones.
How lumpen Danish sounded next to it.
Then outside to the usual polar sun,
boring through the head. The *Pilot* says:

'At Uummannaq, at 70°41'N, broccoli and radishes
grow well and turnips, lettuce and chervil
sometimes succeed.' For days I can think only
of failed lettuces.

Uummannaq – a sound like the mind growing
closer to itself. On the ship, we ate less grandly
laughing at jokes more petitions for understanding.
There, dawn was never unwitnessed and
we rectified our days with hours
that passed in long black waves, like slicks.

In the Ilulissat hotel rich Danes eat
musk ox braised on an iceberg terrace;
half-tame huskies, kept for scenery,
do the rounds, begging. At the tables,
huddled couples eat in unsmiling silence.
The sun sinks until it is a red-flare iceberg.
The dogs squeal at the extinguishing
of its dark fire.

Current

'The West Greenland Current (1.136) sets N along the coast, with a maximum rate of about ½ knot, and does not appear to enter Disko Bugt until midsummer, when the flow of melted water from the coastal areas encourages an inflow.'

The hot bite of thought
is never far from our minds.

Like the sour whortleberry
which promises only hunger.

Clumps of night.
Suddenly nothing is enough
time becomes
a neutral famine.
The sky a dark pastel, grey and ochre.

'The entrance is encumbered with islands and dangers, but there are deep channels between shoal water in the SE part of the bight'

To be swallowed by the slab surge
of ice. The drawl
of Spartan luxury.
We are all men here. So far north now, although August and
still the sun.

•

Depths

'Unlike most of the banks off the W coast of Greenland, the E part of Disko Bank is very uneven and a number of isolated dangers lie on it.'

The *Pilot* tells us to beware
the Porsil Grund – a rock invisible
beneath the surface. The ship scours the seabed
for depths, troughs, channels, ruts –
evidence of past glaciations when the Ice Age
scraped across the ocean floor.

The depths see us, a seabound dirigible,
puncturable, transient, much as the ice
takes no notice at all
of our passing.

On the ship
night draws in.
I wonder
will I remember to remove myself
before the voyage home.

Kap Farvel*

It starts with endings. The Greenlandic name is
Nunaap Isua; hear how it flows
without edges. From our charts spill
sleek cities of nothing bearing us toward the end.
Torssukatak. Mountains to starboard –
some cruel republic of shale
and regret. *Satsigsuarqat*
Landlife seems inelegant, now, with its cache
of streets and mud and shops. *Tasiussassuaq*
We make good our course. Here
confessions won't help us. *Oqutalik*
Only ringing blue and white spears of
light – time running down then
a return to darkness.

*In English, Cape Farewell